Mark Wahlberg

From Music to Movies , A Hollywood Journey

Copyright

All rights reserved. No part of this publication may be reproduced, distributed, or transmitted in any form or by any means, including photocopying, recording, and other electronic or mechanical methods, without prior written permission of the publisher, except in case of briefs quotation embodied in critical reviews and certain other noncommercial uses permitted by copyright law.

Copyright © Benny M. Williams,2024

Table of content

Introduction

Chapter 1:Early Years and Family Background

The Rise to Fame

Chapter 2:Career in Hollywood

Entrepreneurship and Business Ventures

Chapter 3:Personal Life

Chapter 4:Challenges and Controversies

Legacy and Influence

Conclusion

Introduction

Mark Wahlberg's rise to prominence is a fascinating tale of transformation, perseverance, and reinvention. From his early years as a troubled child in Boston to becoming one of Hollywood's most sought-after actors and businesspeople, Wahlberg has reinvented himself several times during his career. His transformation from "Marky Mark" rapper to an award-winning actor and successful businessman has established him as a one-of-a-kind character in the entertainment industry. Wahlberg's career has spanned decades, and he has worked in a variety of fields, including music, acting, production, and business, all while developing a brand that embodies his own values and work ethic.

Mark Robert Michael Wahlberg was born on June 5, 1971, in Boston, Massachusetts, and grew up in a working-class neighbourhood filled with hardships that shaped his character. He rose to prominence in the early 1990s as the vocalist of the hip-hop group Marky Mark and the Funky Bunch, best known for their smash single "Good Vibrations." Despite his early success in music, Wahlberg encountered personal challenges, including legal troubles and time in prison, forcing him to confront his demons and change his course.

His switch to acting was a watershed moment in his career. Wahlberg established his talent in the 1990s with roles in films such as Boogie Nights (1997), in which he played the porn star Dirk Diggler, a performance that demonstrated his breadth as an actor and gained him critical acclaim. His filmography grew over the years, with major performances in films such as The Fighter (2010), The Departed (2006), and Ted (2012), cementing his place among the elite in Hollywood.

However, Wahlberg's story extends beyond his time in front of the camera. His enterprising zeal drove him to pursue a variety of business enterprises, including the hugely successful Wahlburgers chain, which became a symbol of his family's values and work ethic. His forays into production and media, most notably as a producer on the successful show Entourage, solidified his position as a Hollywood power figure.

In addition to his professional accomplishments, Wahlberg is well-known for his humanitarian initiatives, particularly in education and community development. His personal life, which includes his marriage to model Rhea Durham and their four children, has been a significant part of his tale, demonstrating his dedication to family and faith.

Mark Wahlberg's rise from a wayward adolescent to one of Hollywood's most powerful and versatile figures is a motivational story of determination. His capacity to constantly reinvent himself has made him a role model for everyone looking to overcome adversity and live a successful, diverse life. Wahlberg is now not only a popular actor and producer but also a successful businessman and philanthropist, establishing a lasting impact in entertainment and beyond.

Chapter 1: Early Years and Family Background

Mark Wahlberg's early life was heavily influenced by both his surroundings and the family relationships that defined his childhood. Mark was born on June 5, 1971, in Boston, Massachusetts. He grew up in the Dorchester district, which is recognized for its working-class roots and rough, urban mentality. He was the youngest of nine children born to Alma Wahlberg, a nurse's aide and waitress, and Donald Wahlberg, a former delivery driver and combat veteran. His family's financial troubles were a constant presence in his life, and the dynamics of growing up in such a large, financially strapped household paved the way for many of the challenges he would encounter later.

Mark's father, Donald, had a huge influence on the family, yet he was frequently absent due to personal concerns, notably alcoholism. Alma, on the other hand, was a caring and diligent matriarch who played an important role in rearing her children. Her influence was profound, and she instilled in Mark and his siblings the values of family, hard work, and tenacity. Despite the hardship in the family home, Alma remained a continuous source of stability, especially as she balanced her career and the obligations of parenting nine children on her own following her divorce from Donald.

The Wahlberg children experienced numerous problems as they grew up, particularly in an area beset by poverty and crime. As the youngest in the family, Mark was exposed to a wide range of experiences that shaped his outlook on life. His elder siblings, particularly his brother Donnie, who was already rising to prominence as a member of the successful boy band New Kids on the Block, served as role models for him in their unique ways. While Donnie was navigating the world of fame and entertainment, Mark was battling to develop his own identity, frequently feeling pressured to live up to the expectations of his family's name.

Throughout his childhood and teens, Mark became involved in a variety of activities that would eventually affect his route to stardom. He was not focused on academics, and his problems at school were frequently exacerbated by behavioural concerns. He attended various Boston-area schools but was frequently expelled or disciplined. During his adolescence, he struggled with authority and lacked a sense of purpose, leading him down a dark path. Mark was involved in petty crime at the age of 13, and things worsened as he approached his mid-teen years. He gained notoriety for his involvement in street fights, drug use, and other dangerous actions. He was once charged with assault and spent time in a correctional facility, which served as a watershed moment in his life.

Mark was 15 years old when he participated in a racially motivated assault on two Vietnamese men in 1986, an incident that would plague him for years. He was arrested and sentenced to two years in prison but only served 45 days. This occurrence was a watershed moment in his life, forcing him to reevaluate his decisions and his future. His time in prison served as a wake-up call, and he understood he needed to make changes in his life. During this period of self-reflection, Mark began to consider an alternative path—one that would eventually lead to music, acting, and success.

Following his release, Mark pursued music, following in the footsteps of his older brother Donnie. In the early 1990s, he joined the hip-hop group Marky Mark and the Funky Bunch, which launched his career. The group's smash record "Good Vibrations" was a huge success, catapulting Mark into the spotlight as "Marky Mark." This period of triumph in the music business was not without its hurdles. Mark was still adjusting to the trappings of celebrity, and his past mistakes, particularly his role in the assault, continued to plague him in public. However, he used his platform to demonstrate that he was capable of more than his previous reputation.

Mark Wahlberg's early years, marked by hardship, disobedience, and the consequences of his choices, eventually laid the groundwork for his change. His time in troubled settings, engagement in crime, and the hardships he had growing up in a difficult environment all helped him develop the resilience he needed to achieve. These early experiences shaped the man he would become: someone who could reinvent himself and overcome adversity to become one of Hollywood's most successful performers and businesspeople. His narrative is one of redemption, demonstrating that no matter how difficult the beginning, a person can always change their course.

The Rise to Fame

Mark Wahlberg's ascent to prominence is a remarkable story of reinvention, perseverance, and grabbing opportunities at critical junctures. Wahlberg's rise to prominence began in the music industry, but it was his move into acting that defined his career and established him as one of Hollywood's most varied and successful characters.

After being released from prison in the late 1980s, Mark was resolved to change the course of his life. At the time, his older brother Donnie Wahlberg had already achieved success as a member of the very popular boy band New Kids on the Block. Mark was inspired and motivated to pursue a career in entertainment after seeing his sibling's success. In 1990, he formed the hip-hop group Marky Mark and the Funky Bunch, which marked his debut in the music industry. The group's success came in 1991 when they released their debut album, Music for the People, which included the hit track "Good Vibrations." The song became an instant hit, rocketing to the top of the charts and establishing Mark's place in the music industry.

"Good Vibrations" was more than just a catchy song; it was a watershed point in Mark's early career, cementing him as a pop culture icon and garnering him the nickname "Marky Mark." His strong appearance, street-smart character, and boyish charm made him a fan favourite, and his success in the music industry helped him shed part of the troublesome reputation that had followed him since his youth. Despite his success in music, Mark soon recognized that his true interest was on the big screen. He began to explore possibilities to make the transition from musician to actor, and his desire led him down a path that would forever alter the trajectory of his life.

Wahlberg made his acting debut in the 1994 film Renaissance Man, which was directed by Penny

Marshall. Although the picture was not a huge success, it was a significant step forward for Wahlberg. His performance drew the attention of Hollywood producers and directors, paving the way for larger parts. Mark's second big break came in 1997, with the film Boogie Nights, directed by Paul Thomas Anderson. In this film, Wahlberg plays Dirk Diggler, a young man who aspires to be a famous porn actor in the 1970s. The picture was a critical success and a turning point in Mark's career. His performance was universally praised for its depth and complexity, demonstrating talent much beyond what was expected of a former pop star.

The success of Boogie Nights demonstrated to both critics and viewers that Mark Wahlberg was a genuine actor with extraordinary versatility. He was no longer just "Marky Mark," the rapper-turned-actor; he was a true Hollywood star. The part won him multiple award nominations and signalled the start of a string of successful films. Wahlberg's ability to transition from a playful, young image to a more sophisticated and sombre character demonstrated his adaptability and willingness to take chances.

Following Boogie Nights, Wahlberg solidified his place as a rising star. He appeared in The Big Hit (1998), an action-comedy that showcased his ability to blend humour and action, as well as the science fiction thriller Planet of the Apes (2001), which highlighted his popularity in big-budget roles. However, it wasn't until the mid-2000s that Wahlberg found his groove. His performance in Martin Scorsese's The Departed (2006), a dark criminal thriller about Boston gangsters, proved to be another career-defining event. The film boasted a star-studded cast, including Leonardo DiCaprio, Matt Damon, and Jack Nicholson, but Wahlberg's performance of Sergeant Dignam, a tough-talking and ethically dubious figure, stood out and won him an Oscar nod for Best Supporting Actor.

By this point, Wahlberg had established himself as one of Hollywood's most in-demand actors. His ability to portray both dramatic and humorous roles with equal success made him a valuable commodity in an industry that frequently types individuals based on their previous triumphs. His second big break came with the release of the smash comedy Ted (2012), in which he acted alongside a CGI-animated teddy bear voiced by Seth MacFarlane. The picture was a commercial success, grossing more than $500 million worldwide, and reinforced Wahlberg's reputation as a versatile leading actor capable of carrying both comic and action films.

Wahlberg's ascent to prominence was distinguished not only by his excellent acting career but also by his ability to spread his influence beyond the screen. He rose to prominence as an entrepreneur, with significant accomplishments including the Wahlburgers restaurant chain, a family business that grew into a successful reality TV show. His efforts to produce films and television shows also allowed him to keep a presence behind the camera, solidifying his status as a Hollywood power figure.

Wahlberg encountered various hurdles on his path to success, including his troubled youth and criticism from those who questioned his ability to switch from music to acting. But, through hard work, determination, and an unwavering will to achieve, Mark Wahlberg defied his doubters, becoming a multifaceted figure with a long-lasting impact on both Hollywood and popular culture.

Mark Wahlberg's rise from a difficult youth to stardom demonstrates his capacity to adapt, change, and seize new possibilities. His ascent to prominence was not sudden but the product of years of hard effort, taking chances and pushing the boundaries of what people expected of him. Today, he is celebrated not only for his acting career, but also for his business success, philanthropy, and unshakable dedication to his family and faith. His climb to prominence is one of Hollywood's most uplifting tales of transformation and rebirth.

Chapter 2:Career in Hollywood

Mark Wahlberg's Hollywood career is a riveting story of growth, perseverance, and extraordinary achievement. From a turbulent upbringing to one of Hollywood's most diverse and recognized performers, Wahlberg's career has been distinguished by calculated risks, imaginative reinventions, and the ability to succeed in a range of genres, including drama, comedy, and action. His professional trajectory displays not just his acting abilities, but also his entrepreneurial enterprises, production work, and long-lasting influence in the industry.

After shedding his "Marky Mark" reputation in the music industry, Wahlberg's early Hollywood jobs centred on proving himself as a respectable actor. The film Boogie Nights (1997), directed by Paul Thomas Anderson, represented a turning point in his career. Wahlberg's performance as

Dirk Diggler, a guy navigating the highs and lows of the 1970s adult film industry, revealed a level of acting aptitude that startled those who knew him as a pop star. The film's popularity and his praised performance earned him critical acclaim and laid the groundwork for his transition to more serious and complicated roles. Wahlberg's performance was acclaimed for its genuine emotional depth, demonstrating his ability to transcend his public persona and play nuanced roles. This picture established him as a starring man in Hollywood, earning him multiple award nominations, including a Golden Globe.

Following the success of Boogie Nights, Wahlberg went on to play a variety of parts that demonstrated his acting abilities. In the 1999 film Three Kings, directed by David O. Russell, he played a soldier during the Gulf War, marking a notable turn toward action and military-themed plays. The film, which examined the greed and corruption of war, was a critical and commercial triumph, with

Wahlberg's performance being hailed for its intensity and conviction. His relationship with filmmaker David O. Russell continued in I Heart Huckabees (2004), a quirky philosophical comedy in which Wahlberg's character questions the meaning of existence. This one-of-a-kind role demonstrated Wahlberg's versatility as an actor by allowing him to play unorthodox and unexpected parts.

However, Wahlberg's performance in The Departed (2006) established his reputation as one of Hollywood's top actors. Martin Scorsese directed this crime thriller, which had a star-studded ensemble cast including Leonardo DiCaprio, Matt Damon, and Jack Nicholson. Sergeant Dignam, played by Wahlberg, is a strong, foul-mouthed cop who provides both comic relief and moral ambiguity in the film's dramatic plot. His portrayal won him critical acclaim and an Oscar nomination for Best Supporting Actor. The film went on to win multiple Oscars, including Best Picture, marking a pinnacle in Wahlberg's career.

Following The Departed, Wahlberg established himself at the vanguard of Hollywood films that combined action, comedy, and drama. In the late 2000s and early 2010s, he starred in a series of films that not only helped him financially but also demonstrated his ability to thrive in a variety of genres. Max Payne (2008), an action-packed video game adaptation, drew on his experience as a leading actor in fast-paced, exhilarating films. Although the film got mixed reviews, Wahlberg's performance as the titular character, a disturbed ex-cop on a revenge quest, was hailed as a standout.

In 2010, Wahlberg produced and acted in The Fighter, a biographical sports drama about boxer Micky Ward. David O. Russell directed the film, which received critical acclaim and was a huge hit. Wahlberg plays Ward, a warrior trying to find his path while coping with family issues. The film awarded Christian Bale an Academy Award for Best Supporting Actor, but Wahlberg's performance was equally praised for its honesty and passion. The Fighter not only adds another critically lauded performance to Wahlberg's resume but also demonstrates his burgeoning presence behind the camera as a producer.

Wahlberg starred in Ted, a Seth MacFarlane-directed comedy that was a huge commercial hit. Playing against a CGI-animated teddy bear, Wahlberg brought his charisma and comedic timing to the part, resulting in an unexpected hit and cementing his place as one of Hollywood's top comedy actors. Ted grossed more than $500 million worldwide and spawned a sequel, Ted 2 (2015), demonstrating Wahlberg's ability to handle blockbuster comedies while maintaining a lucrative career in action pictures.

In the mid-2010s, Wahlberg's career moved beyond acting, and he became a more renowned producer. His production firm, Closest to the Hole Productions, began producing successful films and television series. Entourage (2004-2011), a sitcom partially based on his journey to

Hollywood prominence, was among his production credits. The show chronicled the fictional career of actor Vincent Chase and his entourage, and it became a cultural sensation. Wahlberg's role in the show's success highlighted his Hollywood influence and entrepreneurial zeal.

Wahlberg has also dabbled with business, starting and running several profitable ventures. One of his most prominent projects is the Wahlburgers restaurant chain, which he created with his brothers Donnie and Paul. The family-run business was turned into a reality TV show, Wahlburgers, which cemented his reputation as a businessman and family man. His entrepreneurial success extended to his work as a co-owner of the sports nutrition company Performance Inspired, as well as his engagement in a variety of real estate transactions, all of which contributed to his diverse career.

Wahlberg's career trajectory exemplifies his adaptability and willingness to reinvent himself as an actor and entrepreneur. His adaptability has enabled him to thrive in a variety of Hollywood roles, from appearing in large blockbusters like Transformers: Age of Extinction (2014) to playing smaller, more tragic roles in films such as The Gambler. His ability to excel in both high-budget action pictures and award-winning dramas has made him a sought-after commodity in an industry that frequently favours performers who can do either.

Mark Wahlberg is currently one of Hollywood's most powerful and successful individuals. His career exemplifies a dynamic combination of raw talent, business acumen, and an unwavering work ethic that has allowed him to flourish both in front and behind the camera. His transformation from former rapper to recognized actor and entrepreneur demonstrates his capacity to change and remain relevant in an ever-changing entertainment industry.

Entrepreneurship and Business Ventures

Mark Wahlberg's entrepreneurship and commercial initiatives are an important part of his legacy, demonstrating his drive, vision, and ability to translate his Hollywood fame into profitable economic prospects. Wahlberg has successfully expanded into several areas, including food, fitness, real estate, and sports nutrition, transforming his brand into a profitable commercial empire. His entrepreneurial energy has been a motivating force behind many of his post-Hollywood initiatives, which have been distinguished by strategic judgments, partnerships, and a dedication to long-term success.

One of Wahlberg's most well-known business initiatives is the Wahlburgers restaurant franchise. Wahlburgers was launched in 2011 by Mark, his brothers Donnie, and Paul. The family-run business began with a simple idea: to provide the public with a high-quality, casual dining experience based on gourmet burgers. The Wahlburgers brand flourished swiftly due to its unique combination of high-quality food and the Wahlberg family's celebrity status. Wahlberg's position in the business was critical, as he helped to build the brand by opening multiple outlets in the United States and abroad. The restaurant chain's success was aided by the reality TV show Wahlburgers (2014-2019), which aired on A&E and chronicled the family's journey to build the business. The show not only made Wahlburgers a household name, but it also boosted Wahlberg's reputation as a successful entrepreneur.

Beyond Wahlburgers, Wahlberg has made considerable investments in other industries, notably real estate. He is well-known for his passion for luxury houses and has spent many years buying, selling, and developing real estate. Wahlberg's real estate portfolio comprises a variety of high-end residences, and he has frequently made news for his astounding multi million-dollar houses. His real estate assets have helped him diversify his wealth and build a strong financial base in addition to his acting and producing career.

Wahlberg has also been involved in the fitness business, specifically with investments in sports nutrition. In 2017, he collaborated with Performance Inspired, a sports nutrition firm co-founded by former professional athletes. The company offers a wide range of products, including protein powders, energy bars, and vitamins, and caters to the health-conscious consumer who values exercise and general well-being. Wahlberg's involvement with the company increased the brand's awareness, and he became a vocal advocate for healthy living and physical exercise, linking the brand with his own lifestyle and public persona.

Wahlberg's entrepreneurial activities have gone beyond fitness and food to include digital media. He co-founded Mark Wahlberg Media, a media company that has created content in a variety of formats, including internet series and reality shows. This venture is consistent with Wahlberg's larger aim of using his brand to reach a worldwide audience. The organization has worked to create unique material for platforms such as YouTube and Instagram, reinforcing his status as a content creator and influencer.

Wahlberg's commercial acumen includes investments in technology. He has invested in several software businesses and apps, believing in the power of technology to disrupt sectors and offer new opportunities. His strategic investments in these industries represent his forward-thinking approach to business, which seeks out new trends and breakthroughs that coincide with his long-term goals.

Another notable business initiative was his partnership with the famed online training platform F45 Training, a global fitness franchise that provides high-intensity group workouts.

Wahlberg became an investor and brand advocate for F45, which helped the company expand its reach and franchise network. Wahlberg's engagement with F45 demonstrates his love for exercise and good living, as well as his ability to spot emerging trends in the health and wellness industry.

Wahlberg's entrepreneurial pursuits not only helped him develop a corporate empire but also solidified his reputation as a hardworking, motivated guy who strives for success in all aspects of his life. His ability to transition easily from entertainment to business illustrates his numerous talents, and his investments in a variety of industries have ensured his financial success even as his acting career slows.

Beyond the concrete parts of his economic empire, Wahlberg's brand has contributed significantly to the success of his companies. His work ethic, disciplined lifestyle, and dedication to family and community have made him an approachable figure for millions of people throughout the world, and he has expertly exploited his celebrity to promote and elevate his numerous business interests. Wahlberg's endeavours have demonstrated that he is more than simply a Hollywood actor; he is also a knowledgeable businessman who knows the importance of brand-building and diversification.

Wahlberg's venture into business exemplifies his adaptability and determination, demonstrating that success in Hollywood is only the beginning of new prospects. His ongoing success as an entrepreneur and investor has cemented his status as one of the most important and ambitious figures in the entertainment industry today. As he grows, it is evident that Wahlberg's economic pursuits will remain a cornerstone of his legacy, amplifying his influence both in and out of the spotlight.

Chapter 3:Personal Life

Mark Wahlberg's personal life is just as dynamic and diverse as his business, providing insight into the evolution of a man who has worked diligently to reinvent himself both in and out of the spotlight. His transformation from a troubled youth to a highly successful actor, producer, entrepreneur, and philanthropist was characterized by resilience, hard effort, and a strong sense of responsibility to his family, faith, and community. Despite being one of Hollywood's most well-known celebrities, Wahlberg has managed to live a reasonably modest and grounded life, putting his values and commitment to the family at the heart of everything he does.

Wahlberg was born on June 5, 1971, in Boston, Massachusetts, as the youngest of nine children. Wahlberg's youth was difficult, as his family struggled financially and he grew up in a harsh Dorchester neighborhood. He has frequently discussed the difficulties of growing up in a working-class community where violence and suffering were commonplace. Mark's early years were distinguished by engagement in small crimes and encounters with the police. As a teenager, Wahlberg was arrested several times, and he even spent time in 1986 for a racially motivated assault. This phase in his life was marked by recklessness and poor decision-making, but he now sees it as a time of learning and progress.

Wahlberg's transition began in the early 1990s, when he sought refuge in music, joining the band Marky Mark and the Funky Bunch as frontman. His brief music career helped him achieve public exposure and laid the groundwork for his subsequent acting career. However, it was not just his career in the entertainment sector that constituted a watershed moment in his life. Wahlberg's choice to move on from his turbulent past and focus on creating a brighter future was driven by his growing faith and desire for personal redemption. He has been outspoken about his spiritual troubles and ultimate conversion to Catholicism, which he credits with allowing him to overcome many of his previous faults. His faith has remained fundamental to his life, with Wahlberg frequently emphasizing the value of prayer, humility, and thanks in his daily life.

The Wahlberg family has been a constant source of encouragement for Mark throughout his life, and his strong family values have served as a guiding factor in both his personal and professional life. Growing up in a large family of eight siblings, Wahlberg developed a strong feeling of loyalty and connection to the people around him. His tight relationship with his mother, Alma Wahlberg, was very important since she influenced his work ethic and beliefs. Alma, who died in 2021, was a pivotal influence in Mark's life, and he has frequently discussed the significant impact she had on him, both personally and professionally. Mark's relationship with his brothers, particularly Donnie Wahlberg, has been a significant influence. Donnie, a member of the boy band New Kids on the Block and a prominent actor, has a close brotherly relationship with Mark. The two have been supportive of one another throughout their careers and frequently work together on commercial endeavours such as the family-run Wahlburgers restaurant chain. This sense of familial loyalty extends to Mark's children, whom he considers his greatest achievements. His relationship with his wife, Rhea Durham, and their four children—Ella Rae, Michael, Brendan, and Grace—has been central to his personal life. Wahlberg is a dedicated father, describing fatherhood as one of the most transformational experiences of his life. Despite his hectic job, he prioritizes spending time with his family, frequently posting about his children on social media and sharing the joys of parenthood. His children provide not just love and delight, but also inspiration, as he seeks to set a good example for them.

Mark's connection with his wife, Rhea Durham, whom he married in 2009, has been an important part of his personal life. Durham, a former model, and Wahlberg have been together for more than 20 years, and their relationship is typically described as one based on mutual respect, love, and understanding. The couple has four children together, and Wahlberg has constantly said that his family is his top focus. Despite their prominence, Wahlberg and Durham have kept their family life very private, preferring to keep their children out of the spotlight as much as possible. Wahlberg frequently discusses the value of being a good husband and father, and he has made a concerted effort to maintain a work-life balance despite the demands of his profession. His relationship with Durham is built on common ideals, and Wahlberg credits her with making him a better person and parent.

Beyond his family, Wahlberg is quite interested in the larger community. He has utilized his position to support organizations that are important to him, notably those that help poor youngsters. Wahlberg, who knows personally the difficulties of growing up in a low-income neighborhood, is dedicated to assisting others in similar situations. His Wahlberg Foundation, established in 2001, has played an important role in supporting a variety of humanitarian efforts, particularly those related to education and youth development. Wahlberg has also been involved in various humanitarian endeavours, including collaborations with the Boys & Girls Clubs of America and the Dana-Farber Cancer Institute. His humanitarian efforts are part of a larger mission to make a positive difference in the world, and he has stated that his philanthropic work is equally important to him as his business ventures and acting career.

Wahlberg's personal life is likewise marked by a dedication to health and fitness. As a well-known fitness enthusiast, he has frequently shared his tough workout regimens with his fans, encouraging them to live a healthy, disciplined, and physically active lifestyle. His commitment to fitness is more than just keeping his physique for aesthetic reasons; it also reflects his work ethic and mental resilience. Wahlberg's passion for fitness has informed several of his business initiatives, most notably his investments in sports nutrition with firms such as Performance Inspired and his engagement with the F45 fitness franchise. Fitness is a significant part of his everyday life, and he has frequently stated that it helps him maintain focus, discipline, and mental clarity, all of which are critical components of his success.

Mark Wahlberg's personal life is defined by his perseverance, dedication to his faith and family, and desire to grow as a person. Wahlberg's journey from turbulent beginnings to becoming one of Hollywood's most recognized performers and businesses has been one of personal growth and transformation. Despite his fame and money, he remains grounded and firmly linked to his roots, always remembering where he came from and seeking to help others. His personal life, which is centred on family, faith, and community service, exemplifies the man he has become—someone who values hard work, loyalty, and the significance of living a balanced and fulfilling life.

Philanthropy and Charitable Work

Mark Wahlberg's humanitarian endeavours are strongly anchored in his personal experiences, from his difficult beginnings in a rough area in Boston to his ascent to fame as an actor and businessman. His path has influenced his view of the value of giving back and using his platform to support causes he cares about. Wahlberg's charitable contributions include a wide range of topics, including youth development, education, health, military veterans, addiction treatment, and worldwide humanitarian initiatives. He is dedicated to leaving a lasting legacy, not just via his riches and resources, but also by sharing his personal story to encourage and motivate others to do the same.

One of the most important components of Wahlberg's philanthropy is his involvement with organizations that help at-risk youngsters. Growing up in a rough neighbourhood, Wahlberg witnessed firsthand the challenges that many young people endure in terms of education, crime, and opportunity. He attributes his achievement to the encouragement he received from mentors, his family, and members of his community who helped him turn his life around. As a result, he has focused much of his philanthropic efforts on assisting young people in similar circumstances. Wahlberg's The Wahlberg Foundation, which he started in 2001, has supported a variety of activities aimed at providing educational resources, mentorship, and career readiness programs to disadvantaged youngsters. The foundation has also granted scholarships to students who do not have the financial resources to attend college, allowing them to pursue their aspirations and break the cycle of poverty.

In addition to his foundation, Wahlberg is heavily involved with the Boys & Girls Clubs of America, a non-profit organization that offers after-school programming and safe spaces for children and teenagers. Wahlberg has worked as a spokesperson for the charity, using his profile to generate awareness and cash for its initiatives. His support for the Boys & Girls Clubs extends beyond financial contributions; he is actively involved in their fundraising activities and frequently speaks about the organization's good impact on the lives of young people. Wahlberg believes strongly in the power of mentorship and the significance of equipping young people with the tools they need to thrive, which is why he has continually sponsored youth-focused organizations.

Wahlberg is also passionate about health issues, notably cancer research and treatment. Wahlberg has a personal connection to cancer since several people close to him have faced the illness. He has been especially engaged in promoting pediatric cancer research and treatment, recognizing how devastating disease can be for children and their families. Wahlberg is a prominent supporter of the Dana-Farber Cancer Institute, a leading cancer research and treatment institution. Over the years, he has leveraged his celebrity profile to collect donations for the organization and has taken part in many events to promote awareness about cancer research. He has also personally donated significant sums to the centre, indicating his dedication to finding cures for cancer and assisting people affected by it.

Wahlberg's devotion to cancer research extends beyond monetary donations, as he uses his voice to encourage others to participate. He has taken part in public awareness initiatives, collaborated with other celebrities to raise donations, and discussed his own cancer experiences via interviews and social media. His efforts have raised millions of dollars for cancer research, contributing to the ongoing battle against the disease. Wahlberg's charity activity in this field demonstrates his strong empathy and commitment to improving the lives of those impacted by cancer.

In addition to his work with children and cancer, Wahlberg is an avid supporter of veterans' organizations. Wahlberg, an advocate for the Wounded Warrior Project, has raised awareness about the difficulties that wounded warriors experience when they return to normal life. He has spoken out on the need for more resources for veterans, notably in the areas of mental health, physical rehabilitation, and career reintegration. Wahlberg has utilized his platform to draw attention to veterans' problems and emphasize the need to give them the resources they require to rehabilitate and rebuild their lives. His involvement with the Wounded Warrior Project includes financial contributions, fundraising events, and public campaigning to ensure that soldiers receive the care and respect they deserve.

Wahlberg's support of veteran charities extends beyond the Wounded Warrior Project. He has also contributed to The Fisher House Foundation, which offers temporary accommodation for military families while their loved ones receive medical treatment. Wahlberg has a profound personal respect for individuals who have served in the military, and he has frequently discussed the sacrifices that veterans make for the greater good. His efforts to help veterans are part of a larger commitment to give back to those who have made sacrifices for others, and he remains an advocate for military-related issues.

Mark Wahlberg's charity influence extends to global humanitarian initiatives. He has actively participated in disaster relief operations, notably following natural catastrophes such as the Haiti earthquake and Hurricane Katrina. Wahlberg has made financial contributions to organizations such as the Red Cross and the World Food Programme, which aid in disaster relief efforts. His gifts have helped to provide food, water, medical supplies, and other necessities to underserved populations. Wahlberg's commitment to disaster relief reflects his belief in the power of aiding people during times of distress, no matter where they are in the world.

Wahlberg's charitable efforts also involve funding addiction recovery clinics. Wahlberg, who has fought with addiction in the past, is committed to assisting others who are struggling with substance misuse. He has been candid about his journey to sobriety and has used his experience to encourage others to seek assistance. Wahlberg has sponsored organizations that provide rehabilitation services, addiction recovery programs, and mental health support, frequently speaking out about the need to obtain treatment and the benefits of a sober lifestyle. His personal experience with addiction has affected his knowledge of the issues that many in recovery encounter, and he continues to push for services and help for people struggling with substance misuse.

Mark Wahlberg's charity initiatives have had a tremendous impact on both local and worldwide populations. Whether through direct financial support, hands-on involvement, or public advocacy, he has utilized his success to promote causes that are important to him and to benefit others. Wahlberg's philanthropic efforts reflect his strong belief in the power of giving back and his desire to make the world a better place. His charity actions have not only benefited individuals and organizations but have also encouraged others to become engaged and make a difference in their communities. For Wahlberg, generosity is more than just money; it's about leveraging his platform to generate long-term change and motivate others to act.

Chapter 4: Challenges and Controversies

Mark Wahlberg's career and personal life, while generally successful, have not been without problems and controversy. From his early years growing up in a gritty Boston area to his ascent to stardom as a Hollywood star, Wahlberg has experienced numerous challenges, many of which have impacted his public image and how he is seen by the media and the general public. Despite the hurdles, Wahlberg has overcome much of his history to become a hugely successful actor, producer, and entrepreneur, but some of the controversies he faced earlier in his career have persisted in public awareness.

One of the most contentious issues in Wahlberg's early life resulted from his involvement in several illicit activities.

Wahlberg was formerly a member of a group of youngsters who committed acts of violence, harassment, and racial intimidation. One of the most notorious episodes occurred in 1986, when Wahlberg and his pals insulted a group of African American students on a school trip, hurling racial slurs and ridiculing them. A few days later, Wahlberg and his friends were involved in a violent incident with a group of youngsters, for which Wahlberg, then 16, was charged with assault and violence.

In 1988, Wahlberg was involved in another, more serious incident, when he and a gang of his pals attacked two Vietnamese men in a racially tinged assault. Wahlberg was convicted of civil rights breaches and spent 45 days in prison for the assault. The episode became a key component of his criminal record, attracting favourable attention years later. Wahlberg's previous actions, especially racial violence, haunted him for many years, and the media frequently mentioned it while reporting his ascent to prominence.

Wahlberg has publicly addressed his past misdeeds and shown regret for them. In interviews, he acknowledged the hurt he caused, particularly to the victims of violent situations, and freely declared that he has evolved. He has also attempted to make apologies, including issuing a public apology to the guys involved in the 1988 assault, one of whom eventually accepted it. In 2014, Wahlberg requested a pardon for his conviction in the Vietnamese assault case, but his request was met with criticism, with some questioning whether he had exhibited genuine remorse.

The controversy surrounding Wahlberg's previous illegal activities, as well as his subsequent attempts to distance himself from them, has raised questions regarding the concept of redemption and whether a person can truly change after committing such crimes. Many people have commended Wahlberg for his efforts to improve himself, while others have condemned his acts and questioned his sincerity.

This debate has persisted throughout Wahlberg's career, even as he continues to achieve success and respect in Hollywood.

Another major incident that Wahlberg encountered occurred in 2017 when he was involved in a pay disparity dispute over his role in the film All the Money in the World. Following the sexual misconduct charges against Kevin Spacey, the film's director, Ridley Scott opted to reshoot parts of the picture. Wahlberg and his co-star Michelle Williams were summoned back for reshoots. According to reports, Wahlberg was paid $1.5 million for the reshoots, whereas Williams was only paid $80 per day, even though both actors were equally committed. The substantial wage differential sparked widespread outrage, with many citing it as an example of Hollywood's gender pay gap.

The debate over the wage difference prompted significant criticism of Wahlberg's actions, with many viewing them as a microcosm of greater structural concerns of inequality in Hollywood.

Wahlberg initially defended his payment, claiming that it was industry standard, but after public and media pressure, he donated the $1.5 million he received from the reshoots to the Time's Up Legal Defense Fund, which helps those affected by sexual harassment and gender inequality in the workplace. His offering was interpreted as an effort to make apologies and address public concern about salary inequality.

This problem, while ultimately handled with Wahlberg's donation, highlighted fundamental discrepancies in Hollywood, particularly in the remuneration of female performers compared to their male counterparts. Wahlberg's involvement in the incident emphasized how power dynamics and industry standards may lead to unequal treatment of women, a problem that has received attention in recent years, particularly in light of the #MeToo movement.

Furthermore, allegations that Wahlberg is tough to work with on set have had an impact on his public image. Some directors and co-stars have portrayed him as hard-nosed and demanding, with some depicting him as anything but collaborative. One significant instance was during his work on the film The Happening with director M. Night Shyamalan, when Wahlberg struggled with the content and their working relationship was not altogether seamless. Wahlberg has rejected these claims, and many have pointed out that the difficulties were most likely caused by his strong desire to present his best work. However, these instances have periodically appeared in the media as part of his complex public character.

Finally, Wahlberg has received criticism for his role in the growth of his restaurant franchise, Wahlburgers. While the restaurant has seen considerable success, thanks in large part to the Wahlberg brothers' involvement, it has also sparked some controversy. According to reports, the company has suffered financially in various locations, with some outlets blaming the problems on weak management or a lack of a sustainable business strategy. Wahlberg's involvement in the company and its financial issues have periodically been discussed, casting doubt on his entrepreneurial prowess.

Despite these controversies, Wahlberg has continued to achieve success in Hollywood, branching out into production and business activities and becoming a well-known actor and producer. Over time, he has sought to separate himself from his previous acts and conflicts, emphasizing his commitment to reform and desire to be a positive influence. While some of these issues have persisted in the narrative surrounding him, Wahlberg's capacity to adapt, learn from his mistakes, and move on has been critical to his success and ability to maintain his prominent position in the entertainment business. His path reminds us that even individuals who commit mistakes may evolve, grow, and redefine themselves over time.

Legacy and Influence

Mark Wahlberg's legacy and influence extend far beyond his accomplishments as an actor. His transformation from a disturbed adolescent to a successful Hollywood star, entrepreneur, and philanthropist has made him a symbol of personal development and resilience. Wahlberg's influence extends beyond the entertainment business to include his entrepreneurial enterprises, passion for health, and efforts to encourage people through his work ethic and dedication.

Wahlberg has established himself as a leading man in Hollywood through a wide body of work that includes action, drama, comedy, and even production. His early performances in films like Boogie Nights (1997) and The Perfect Storm (2000) received critical acclaim, demonstrating his ability to shift into multifaceted characters. He eventually established his box-office success with huge action pictures such as The Departed (2006), Transformers (2007), and Ted (2012), among others. Wahlberg's ability to consistently select lucrative films and deliver engaging performances has given him a reputation as one of Hollywood's most dependable actors.

However, Wahlberg's influence extends beyond his acting. As a producer, he has contributed to some of the most noteworthy productions in television and movies. Wahlberg's producing company, Wahlberg Brothers, has produced multiple hit television shows, including the popular HBO series Entourage and Boardwalk Empire. His work as a producer has enabled him to help start talents and create content that represents his vision, thus increasing his influence in the entertainment industry.

In addition to his achievements in Hollywood, Wahlberg's entrepreneurial ventures have influenced his legacy. He has established a portfolio of profitable businesses, most notably the Wahlburgers restaurant franchise. The restaurant, which was once a family business with his brothers Paul and Donnie Wahlberg, has developed into a nationwide brand. Wahlberg's economic aptitude and ability to convert a family initiative into a national hit demonstrate that his entrepreneurial passion is just as strong as his acting career.

His commitment to fitness has had a huge impact on his public image and influence. As a fitness enthusiast, Wahlberg has become a role model for many people who want to improve their physical health and wellness. His commitment to working out and living a healthy lifestyle has inspired his brand, and his fitness journey is frequently featured in media and interviews. His shift from a young, rebellious figure to a disciplined, health-conscious person is viewed as another illustration of the personal development that defines his legacy.

Perhaps one of the most striking aspects of Wahlberg's legacy is his capacity to change his life. From his rough childhood and criminal background to his current standing as a Hollywood entrepreneur and philanthropist, Wahlberg's narrative is one of redemption and fortitude. He has become an advocate for second chances, using his position to motivate others to overcome obstacles and achieve their ambitions. Wahlberg's metamorphosis from a former gang member and criminal to an admired public figure exemplifies the strength of personal development and the possibility of change, making his tale one of resilience and hope for people facing misfortune.

Furthermore, Wahlberg's charity efforts have added to his excellent legacy. His humanitarian initiatives, through the Mark Wahlberg Youngsters Foundation, aim to assist impoverished youngsters by providing them with resources and chances to develop brighter futures. His foundation helps to fund a variety of educational and community-based activities, particularly in his birthplace of Boston. Wahlberg has also been involved in various charity activities, such as those that benefit veterans and first responders, both of which he is particularly passionate about.

In terms of cultural influence, Wahlberg's career has interacted with broader cultural movements, demonstrating his significance. His transformation from a rapper in the early 1990s to a respected actor and entrepreneur reflects changes in popular culture and the entertainment industry. Wahlberg embodies the concept of reinvention and has demonstrated how an individual can overcome hurdles to become a more well-rounded, successful person. His ascension from pop star to Hollywood heavyweight has prompted a broader discussion about how celebrities may create and affect cultural norms and expectations.

Wahlberg's work ethic, dedication, and determination have left an indelible mark on the entertainment world. He is noted for his extreme concentration, early morning routines, and dedication to mastering his craft. This effort has garnered him respect from his colleagues and has played a significant role in his continued success. Wahlberg's effect on the next generation of actors and entrepreneurs is clear in the fact that many look to him as a role model, not just for his accomplishments, but also for his ability to stay grounded and committed to his goals in the face of adversity.

Wahlberg has maintained a significant presence on social media, using sites such as Instagram to interact with followers, promote his businesses, and provide insights into his daily life. His ability to connect with audiences, particularly younger generations, has helped him remain relevant in an ever-changing entertainment industry. Wahlberg's social media presence goes beyond personal branding; he routinely uses his platform to spread positive messages about self-improvement, wellness, and hard work.

Overall, Wahlberg's legacy is one of transformation and influence. From his beginnings in the music industry to his current status as an actor, producer, entrepreneur, and philanthropist, Wahlberg has demonstrated that it is possible to develop and redefine oneself throughout time. His ability to adapt to the ever-changing entertainment industry, as well as his commercial enterprises and humanitarian efforts, have solidified his place in Hollywood and popular culture. Wahlberg's life exemplifies the power of reinvention, personal growth, and the impact that one individual can have on the world, especially when they utilize their influence for good.

Conclusion

Mark Wahlberg's life and career tell a fascinating story of redemption, determination, and accomplishment. Wahlberg's journey has been marked by dramatic transition since his poor beginnings in Boston, where he grew up in a difficult neighbourhood and had early encounters with the law. His early past, which included membership in a street gang and criminal activity, may easily have shaped his future. However, Wahlberg bucked the odds, achieving success via his love of music, natural charisma, and unshakable determination to change his life's course.

Wahlberg's career in the entertainment sector began as a member of the early 1990s hip-hop group Marky Mark and the Funky Bunch, where he gained recognition for his songs and daring persona. The success of his singing career gave him a platform, but it was his crossover into acting that cemented his place in Hollywood. Wahlberg's early film appearances, especially his breakout performance in Boogie Nights (1997), showcased his acting versatility and talent. He quickly progressed from pop celebrity to renowned actor, appearing in both highly praised films and big-budget blockbusters. His ability to transition from a musician to a Hollywood leading man was a watershed point in his career, foreshadowing his future success in the industry.

However, Wahlberg's narrative is more than just his filmography. As his acting career progressed, he broadened his horizons by entering into entrepreneurship. His commercial ventures, including the founding of the Wahlburgers restaurant chain, demonstrated his remarkable business acumen and ability to negotiate the difficult world of entrepreneurship. Wahlberg did not simply invest in enterprises for financial benefit; he took an active role, using his celebrity to establish brands and influence markets. His forays into the fitness industry and other businesses demonstrated his adaptability and willingness to expand his profession and grow in new directions.

Beyond business and entertainment, Wahlberg's influence extends to philanthropy. Through the Mark Wahlberg Youngsters Foundation, he has dedicated himself to giving chances to at-risk youngsters, assisting them in achieving their goals through education and mentoring programs. His dedication to philanthropic work, particularly in his hometown of Boston, has had a significant impact on numerous lives, demonstrating his willingness to give back to the community that shaped him. Wahlberg's efforts to help veterans, first responders, and humanitarian groups show a greater sense of duty and compassion for those in need.

Wahlberg's rise to prominence has not been without its hurdles and controversy. His early engagement in criminal activity, including an assault conviction, is a crucial aspect of his narrative. However, one of the most fascinating features of his legacy is his ability to learn from his failures and use them to fuel personal progress. Wahlberg's desire to accept his sins and work toward atonement has sparked both criticism and acclaim, but it is ultimately a compelling reminder of the value of second chances and the opportunity to transform one's life.

Mark Wahlberg's influence extends far beyond Hollywood and the business world. His dedication to fitness and health has made him a role model for many people, particularly those seeking to develop physical and mental discipline. His strict daily routines and emphasis on living a healthy lifestyle have encouraged a new generation to value fitness and well-being. Wahlberg's ability to modify not only his work but also his entire lifestyle has elevated him to the status of a paragon of tenacity and discipline.

Wahlberg's influence on pop culture is unmistakable. His journey from a turbulent youth to a Hollywood icon is one that many people can relate to, especially those from challenging origins. His success in the entertainment industry, combined with his entrepreneurial enterprises, has solidified his place as one of modern Hollywood's most prominent personalities. His capacity to stay relevant in a quickly changing business, his dedication to personal and professional development, and his entrepreneurial spirit have distinguished him as a true 21st-century Renaissance Man.

Mark Wahlberg's biography finally demonstrates persistence, flexibility, and achievement. His capacity to reinvent himself throughout time, accept new challenges, and overcome personal hurdles, has created his legacy. Wahlberg's metamorphosis from a young rebel to a respected actor, businessman, and philanthropist exemplifies the importance of self-reflection, hard effort, and devotion. His tale is an encouragement to people who encounter difficulties, demonstrating that with determination, anyone can change their path and make a positive difference in the world.

Finally, Mark Wahlberg's life exemplifies the power of atonement and the endless opportunities for personal development. From a turbulent youth to a tremendously successful career in Hollywood and elsewhere, Wahlberg's legacy is one of transition and impact. His contributions to the entertainment business, charity initiatives, and entrepreneurial ventures have made a lasting impression on the world. Wahlberg's tale is about more than simply fame and money; it's about overcoming hurdles, creating a brighter future, and motivating others to do the same.

www.ingramcontent.com/pod-product-compliance
Lightning Source LLC
Chambersburg PA
CBHW071110240526
45469CB00006BD/2416